# Commercial diving projects inland/inshore

Diving at Work Regulations 1997

# APPROVED CODE OF PRACTICE

**L104**

**HSE** BOOKS

**The Approved Code of Practice**

This Approved Code of Practice has been approved by the Health and
Safety Commission with the consent of the Secretary of State. It gives
practical advice on how to comply with the law. If you follow the advice
you will be doing enough to comply with the law in respect of those specific
matters on which the Approved Code of Practice gives advice. You may use
alternative methods to those set out in the Approved Code of Practice in
order to comply with the law.

However, the Approved Code of Practice has a special legal status. If you
are prosecuted for breach of health and safety law, and it is proved that you
did not follow the relevant provisions of the Approved Code of Practice, you
will need to show that you have complied with the law in some other way or
a court will find you at fault.

# Contents

By virtue of section 16(1) of the Health and Safety at Work etc Act 1974, and with the consent of the Secretary of State for Environment, Transport and the Regions, the Health and Safety Commission has on 10 December 1997 approved the Code of Practice entitled *Commercial diving projects inland/inshore*.

The Code of Practice is approved for the purposes of providing practical guidance with respect to the requirements of the Diving at Work Regulations 1997 (SI 1997 No 2776) and with respect to regulation 3 of the Management of Health and Safety at Work Regulations 1992 (SI 1992 No 2051). The Code of Practice comes into force on 1 April 1998.

Reference in this Code of Practice to another document does not imply approval by HSC of that document except to the extent necessary to give effect to this Code of Practice.

Signed

ROSEMARY BANNER
*Secretary to the Health and Safety Commission*

19 January 1998

This publication contains the Approved Code of Practice (ACOP) and additional guidance for commercial diving projects inland/inshore, together with the relevant regulations from the Diving at Work Regulations 1997. The full text of the Regulations (SI 1997 No 2776) is available from the Stationery Office.

For convenience, the full text of the Regulations is included in *italic* type, with the accompanying ACOP in **bold** type.

## Explanation and intention of the Approved Code of Practice

1    This Approved Code of Practice (ACOP) (referred to as the Code) gives advice on meeting the requirements of the Diving at Work Regulations 1997 (referred to as the Diving Regulations) for commercial diving projects inland/inshore. In particular, the Code gives advice on how to comply with those Regulations that are set out in general terms.

2    It should not be assumed that compliance with the Diving Regulations means that all aspects of the law are being complied with. The requirements of other legislation may also need to be fulfilled. A list of other major health and safety at work legislation in force when this Code was published is set out in Annex 4.

### Health and safety legislation

3    The basis of health and safety law in Great Britain is the Health and Safety at Work etc Act 1974 (the HSW Act). The HSW Act sets out the general duties that employers and the self-employed have towards employees and members of the public, and the duties that employees have to themselves and to each other. These duties are qualified in the HSW Act by the principle of *so far as is reasonably practicable*.

4    Health and safety regulations are law, approved by Parliament. These are usually made under the HSW Act following proposals from the Health and Safety Commission (HSC). Regulations set out requirements which should be met.

### Scope and areas covered by the Code

5    This Code applies to all diving projects conducted in support of civil engineering or marine-related projects and fish farming:

(a)    inshore within United Kingdom territorial waters adjacent to Great Britain (generally 12 nautical miles from the low water line);

(b)    inland in Great Britain including in docks, harbours, rivers, culverts, canals, lakes, ponds and reservoirs; and

(c)    in tanks or swimming pools.

6    This Code does not apply to:

(a)    scallop diving for which the Health and Safety Executive (HSE) has issued specific guidance material;

(b)    diving projects specifically covered by one of the other Codes approved by HSC under the Diving Regulations.

### Who wrote the Code and how it was agreed

7    Representatives of the Association of Diving Contractors (ADC) worked with HSE to produce a draft Code that was published by HSC in July 1996 for public consultation.

**Updating arrangements**

8    There will be regular discussions between HSE, the ADC and other parties in the industry to discuss the current applicability of the Code. When technology, industry standards or practices change, consideration will be given to amending the Code. All amendments will be the subject of formal public consultation.

**The other diving Codes**

9    There are four other Codes covering diving at work:

(a)    Commercial diving projects offshore (ISBN 978 0 7176 1494 3);

(b)    Media diving projects (ISBN 978 0 7176 1497 4);

(c)    Recreational diving projects (ISBN 978 0 7176 1496 7); and

(d)    Scientific and archaeological diving projects (ISBN 978 0 7176 1498 1).

10    Each of these Codes has been drafted by HSE with the help of the industry associations for the relevant sector and covers standards and practices that are relevant to that sector's particular area of diving.

**Sources of information**

11    The Codes do not cover the detailed technical aspects of controlling the risks from diving at work. Guidance published by HSE provides detailed technical advice on assessing and minimising the risks. Details can be obtained from HSE.

12    Guidance is also published by the ADC, the International Marine Contractors Association (IMCA) (and its predecessor the Association of Offshore Diving Contractors (AODC)) and the Diving Medical Advisory Committee (DMAC). A list giving details of this guidance is set out in Annex 5. You should check that the list is still current.

13    When an ACOP paragraph has an adjacent asterisk (*) this indicates that relevant industry technical guidance is listed in Annex 5. This does not mean, however, that the industry guidance has the legal status of an Approved Code of Practice.

# Definitions in the Regulations

## Regulation 2

Regulation
2(1)

Guide

2(1)

*(1)   "diver" means a person at work who dives;*

14   'At work' means as an employee or as a self-employed person. The phrase covers divers who dive as part of their duties as an employee and divers who are in business on their own account during the time that they devote themselves to work as a self-employed person. Diving does not have to be the main activity of the employee or the self-employed person. The Diving Regulations apply to any diving project when at least one person is at work.

Regulation

2(2)

*(2)   For the purposes of these Regulations a person "dives" if -*

*(a)   he enters -*

*(i)     water or any other liquid; or*

*(ii)    a chamber in which he is subject to pressure greater than
         100 millibars above atmospheric pressure; and*

*(b)   in order to survive in such an environment he breathes in air or other gas
       at a pressure greater than atmospheric pressure.*

Guide

2(2)

15   Environments such as scientific clean rooms or submersible craft subject to an internal pressure of less than 100 millibars above local ambient atmospheric pressure are not covered by the Diving Regulations.

Regulation

2(1)

*(1)   "diving project" means any activity, made up of one or more diving operations, in which at least one person takes part or will take part as a diver and extends from the time when that person, or the first such person, commences to prepare to dive until that person, or the last such person, has left the water, chamber or other environment in which the dive, or any part of the dive, took place and has completed any requisite decompression procedures, including, where it may be reasonably anticipated that this will be needed, any therapeutic recompression.*

Guide

2(1)

16   'Diving project' is the term used for the overall diving job - whether it lasts two hours or two months.

17   A diving project is made up of one or more diving operations.

Regulation
2(1)

*(1)   "diving operation" means a diving operation identified in the diving project plan pursuant to regulation 8(3);*

## Regulation 8

Regulation

8(3)

*(3)   The diving project plan shall identify each diving operation which makes up the diving project and the nature and size of any diving operation so identified shall be such that it can be safely supervised by one person.*

Guide

2(1), 8(3)

18   'Diving operations' can be made up of either a number of dives or even a single dive. A diving operation is the portion of a diving project identified in the diving project plan which can be safely supervised by one supervisor. It will normally be evident what this portion of work is, but factors such as the

task, site conditions and the diving techniques to be used, all contribute to making the decision. For example, a 28-day diving project might be made up of 40 diving operations.

19   The diving contractor has the main responsibility under the Diving Regulations for ensuring that a safe diving project is carried out, although other people have responsibilities under the Diving Regulations, for example clients. The diving contractor should determine, after studying the risk assessment, how many diving operations the diving project is to be broken down into and must appoint a supervisor to supervise each operation. The diving contractor has responsibility for ensuring that all parts of a diving project are managed in such a way as to ensure the safety of the people involved in it. If there is more than one diving operation being conducted at the same time, as part of the diving project, the diving contractor has a responsibility to ensure that there is proper co-ordination.

20   The supervisor has a duty to direct the diving operation safely. If a supervisor does not agree with the size or complexity of the portion of the diving project allocated to him or her as an operation to supervise, the supervisor should raise the matter with the diving contractor. A supervisor should not participate in a diving operation that he or she considers to be unsafe because, for example, in the supervisor's opinion it is too large for one person to supervise safely or that the supervisor knows that he or she is not competent to supervise.

## Regulation 2

*(1)   "the 1995 Order" means the Health and Safety at Work etc. Act 1974 (Application outside Great Britain) Order 1995[a];*

*(a) SI 1995/263*

## Regulation 3

*(2)   These Regulations shall apply to and in relation to the premises and activities outside Great Britain to which sections 1 to 59 and 80 to 82 of the Health and Safety at Work etc. Act 1974 apply by virtue of the 1995 order as they apply within Great Britain.*

21   The Diving Regulations cover all diving projects inland in Great Britain, within territorial waters, as well as oil- and gas-related diving projects (including diving projects involving offshore installations and any preparatory work and pipelines) beyond territorial waters on the UK designated areas of the continental shelf.

*(1)   These Regulations shall apply to and in relation to any diving project apart from the following -*

> *(a)   the care or treatment of patients in a hospital or other place, not under the control of the diving contractor, where emergency medical treatment is provided or in transit to such hospital or place where the means of transit is provided by or in respect of the hospital or other place;*

**Guide**

3(1)(a)

22    The use of hyperbaric chambers within diving projects is covered by the Diving Regulations. However, those receiving hyperbaric treatment at a hospital or other place are outside the scope of the Diving Regulations. This is to avoid duplication of responsibilities when another authority is involved in the medical treatment of a diver.

23    Where hyperbaric treatment is to be provided in a recompression chamber provided by a person other than the diving contractor for that diving project, the arrangements for this should be covered in the diving project plan. The Diving Regulations do not apply to the hyperbaric treatment provided by that other person.

**Regulation**

3(1)(c)

*(1)    These Regulations shall apply to and in relation to any diving project apart from the following -*

*(c)    work carried out in any air which is compressed in order to prevent the ingress of ground water to the works or to stabilise the area around the works.*

**Guide**

3(1)(c)

24    Construction activities that are subject to the Compressed Air Regulations 1996 where the primary purpose is either to keep ground water out or to make a structure stable are not covered by the Diving Regulations.

## Regulation 5

**Regulation**

5(1)

*(1)    No person at work shall dive in a diving project and no employer shall employ any person in such a project unless there is one person and one person only who is the diving contractor for that project.*

**Guide**

5(1)

25    The term 'person' used to identify the diving contractor under this Regulation means a person with legal identity such as an individual or a company and includes a body of people corporate or incorporate.

# Clients and others

*Every person who to any extent is responsible for, has control over or is engaged in a diving project or whose acts or omissions could adversely affect the health and safety of persons engaged in such a project, shall take such measures as it is reasonable for a person in his position to take to ensure that these Regulations are complied with.*

**ACOP**

26    The actions and activities of other people can affect the safety of the dive team even though they are not members of the team, and therefore they may have responsibilities for ensuring that the Regulations are complied with for those matters under their control. These people include:

(a)    the client who has placed a contract with a diving contractor to deliver a diving project. The client may be the owner of a site where diving work is going to take place, or the owner's agent, or a contractor acting on behalf of the owner or agent. If the owner or agent appoints an on-site representative, he or she should be satisfied that that person is competent for the task;

(b)    the principal contractor carrying out work for the client and overseeing the work of the diving contractor;

(c)    a consultant acting for the client, owner, contractor or agent;

(d)    a master of a vessel or floating structure from which diving is to take place who controls the vessel or floating structure and who has overall responsibility for the safety of the vessel or floating structure and all personnel on it;

(e)    any other person whose actions or activities may affect the safety of the diving project.

27    These people should consider carefully the actions required of them to comply with the Diving Regulations. They should, where appropriate:

(a)    take reasonable steps to ensure that any diving contractor selected is capable of complying with the Diving Regulations;

(b)    make available to the diving contractor the results of any risk assessments undertaken by other persons under other statutory legislation that could affect the health and safety of the dive team;

(c)    agree to provide facilities and extend all reasonable support to the supervisor or diving contractor in the event of an emergency. The diving project plan should reflect this;

(d)    consider whether any known underwater or above-water items of plant under their control may cause a hazard to the dive team. Such items may include locks, weirs, water intakes or discharge points causing suction or turbulence, and ship propellers. The diving contractor should be informed of the location and nature of such hazards. They should also provide the diving contractor, in good time, with details of any changes to this information occurring before or during the course of the diving project;

(e) consider whether other activities in the vicinity may affect the safety of the diving project; for example, they may need to arrange for the suspension of loading or unloading of vessels, piling work or demolition activities;

(f) ensure that they have a formal control system in place to cover diving activities, for example, a permit-to-work system;

(g) provide the diving contractor with details of any possible substance likely to be encountered by the dive team that would be a hazard to their health, for example sewage or chemicals. This information should be provided in writing and in sufficient time to allow the diving contractor to carry out the relevant risk assessment and, if necessary, to take appropriate action;

(h) keep the supervisor informed of any changes that may affect the supervisor's diving operation in so far as they have control over or knowledge of such changes; for example, vessel movement in a harbour or on a river, so that diving can be suspended if the diving site is, or may be, endangered.

28 Other groups of people, for example harbour masters, may have authority over the dive under Regulations other than the Diving Regulations.

29 The duty under this regulation extends to diving contractors, supervisors, divers and people involved in the diving project whether directly or indirectly, for example crane operators, lorry drivers, and maintenance personnel. They should ensure that their tasks and how they undertake them do not affect the safety of the dive team.

# Diving contractors

## Regulation 5

Regulation

5

*(1)    No person at work shall dive in a diving project and no employer shall employ any person in such a project unless there is one person and one person only who is the diving contractor for that project.*

*(2)    The diving contractor shall, subject to paragraph (3), be the person who -*

*(a)    is the employer of the diver or divers engaged in the diving project; or*

*(b)    dives in the diving project as a self-employed diver.*

*(3)    Where there is more than one person falling within paragraph (2) those persons shall jointly appoint in writing before the commencement of the diving project one of themselves to act as diving contractor.*

ACOP

5

**30    The Diving Regulations require that one person (see paragraph 25 for definition) is identified as the diving contractor for each diving project. The main duties under the Diving Regulations are placed on the diving contractor. The diving contractor will normally be the employer of the divers engaged in the diving project.**

**31    Where the client engages more than one employer of divers or self-employed diver for the diving project, it must be established and recorded in writing who will be the diving contractor for that project.**

## Regulation 6

Regulation

6(1),(3)(d),(e)

*(1)    The diving contractor shall ensure, so far as is reasonably practicable, that the diving project is planned, managed and conducted in a manner which protects the health and safety of all persons taking part in that project.*

*(3)    The diving contractor shall -*

*(d)    ensure, so far as reasonably practicable, that any person taking part in the diving project complies with the requirements and prohibitions imposed on him by or under the relevant statutory provisions and observes the provisions of the diving project plan;*

*(e)    ensure that a record containing the required particulars is kept for each diving operation;*

ACOP

6(1),(3)(d),(e)

**32    The diving contractor's responsibilities are to ensure that:**

**(a)    the diving project is properly and safely managed;**

**(b)    risk assessments have been carried out (see section 'Diving project plan and risk assessment');**

**(c)    the place from which the diving is to be carried out is suitable and safe;**

(d) a suitable diving project plan is prepared which includes emergency and contingency plans (see section 'Diving project plan and risk assessment');

(e) the supervisor and dive team are fully briefed on the diving operation that they will be involved with and aware of the contents of the overall diving project plan;

(f) there are sufficient personnel in the dive team to enable the diving project to be carried out safely (see section 'Dive teams and associated working practice');

(g) the personnel are competent and/or qualified (see sections 'Supervisors' and 'Divers');

(h) supervisors are appointed in writing and the extent of their control documented (see section 'Supervisors');

(i) where appropriate a suitable mobilisation and familiarisation programme is completed by all the members of the dive team. Other personnel involved in the dive project, for example ship's crew, may also need to complete the programme (see section 'Diving project plan and risk assessment');

(j) adequate arrangements exist for first aid and medical treatment (see section 'Dive teams and associated working practice');

(k) suitable and sufficient plant is provided and that it is correctly certified and maintained (see sections 'Diving plant' and 'Maintenance of diving plant');

(l) as far as they are able, the team is medically fit to dive (see section 'Medical checks');

(m) diving project records are kept containing the required details of the diving project (see Annex 1);

(n) a clear reporting and responsibility structure is laid down in writing;

6(1),(3)(d),(e)

(o) all other relevant regulations are complied with.

## Regulation 7

*(1) No person shall act as a diving contractor unless the particulars listed in Schedule 1 have been supplied in writing to the Executive by or in respect of that person.*

*(2) Where there is a change in any of the particulars supplied under paragraph (1) the diving contractor shall ensure that details of the change are forthwith supplied in writing to the Executive.*

7(1),(2)

33 Before any person (see paragraph 25 for definition) acts as a diving contractor, he or she must ensure that HSE is provided with information about his or her identity and where he or she can be contacted. The diving contractor is also required to inform HSE of any subsequent changes to this information. Full details required are set out in Schedule 1 to the Diving Regulations. HSE will acknowledge receipt of such information.

7(1),(2)

# Diving project plan and risk assessment

## Regulation 6

Regulation

6(2)

*(2)   The diving contractor shall -*

*(a)   ensure that, before the commencement of the diving project, a diving project plan is prepared in respect of that project in accordance with regulation 8 and that the plan is thereafter updated as necessary during the continuance of the project;*

*(b)   before the commencement of any diving operation -*

*(i)   appoint a person to supervise that operation in accordance with regulation 9;*

*(ii)   make a written record of that appointment; and*

*(iii)   ensure that that person is supplied with a copy of any part of the diving project plan which relates to that operation;*

*(c)   as soon as possible after the appointment of a supervisor, provide that supervisor with a written record of his appointment.*

## Regulation 8

Regulation

8(1),(3)

*(1)   The diving project plan shall be based on an assessment of the risks to the health and safety of any person taking part in the diving project and shall consist of a record of the outcome of the planning carried out in accordance with regulation 6(1) including all such information and instructions as are necessary to give advice to and to regulate the behaviour of those so taking part to ensure, so far as is reasonably practicable, their health and safety.*

*(3)   The diving project plan shall identify each diving operation which makes up the diving project and the nature and size of any diving operation so identified shall be such that it can be safely supervised by one person.*

ACOP

34   The diving contractor is responsible for ensuring that a risk assessment is carried out and a diving project plan prepared.

**Risk assessment**

35   A risk assessment must be carried out to identify site-specific hazards and their risks.

36   As a matter of safe working practice, the project risk assessment should be reviewed at regular intervals, even if the risk is minimal, to ensure that the risk assessment is still adequate and does not need to be revised.

37   A risk assessment made under the Diving Regulations will cover, in part, the obligation to make an assessment under the Management of Health and Safety at Work Regulations 1999. There will be no need to repeat those aspects of the assessment, so long as they remain valid, in any other assessment that is carried out. However, all significant risks not covered by the diving project assessment (including risks to members of the public arising from the diving project/diving activities)

6(2), 8(1),(3)

must be covered by the risk assessment carried out under the Management of Health and Safety at Work Regulations 1999 or in any assessment required to be carried out under other specific regulations.

## Diving project plan

38    Based on this information, the diving project plan must state how the hazards identified and risks assessed will be controlled. The diving project plan may include a diving contractor's standard operating rules, including generic risk assessments. All documents should show the date upon which they were prepared. The diving project plan should record the outcome of the planning carried out in preparing the risk assessment including all information and instructions which, so far as is reasonably practicable, are necessary to protect the health and safety of all those taking part in the diving project. It should also explain when and how reviews of the plan, the dive site and the specific risk assessments should be conducted. The results of the review will only need to be recorded if there has been a significant change.

39    The diving project plan must cover the general principles of the diving techniques to be used as well as the needs of the particular operation. It must also provide contingency procedures for any foreseeable emergency, including retrieving injured and/or unconscious divers from the water.

40    Each supervisor must be given a copy of that part of the diving project plan relevant to the diving operation that he or she will be supervising.

41    Some examples of hazards and risks are given in paragraphs 42-72. However, this is not a complete list of all hazards or all measures needed to control risk and in special circumstances, or if certain contingencies arise, more stringent safeguards may be needed.

## General

### Diving methods

42    Diving methods and equipment should be determined as part of the risk assessment.

43    Diving using surface-supplied breathing apparatus is the preferred method of carrying out diving operations under this Code because it is considered to be the safest method of diving for the vast majority of diving operations covered.

44    The diving contractor should ensure as a minimum that:

(a)    the diver wears a full face mask which should be fitted with either an oral nasal or a mouthpiece;

(b)    the diver carries an independent secondary source of breathing gas (for example, a bail-out cylinder);

(c)    there is a lifeline from the diver to the surface. This should be tended. Two divers connected by a buddy line need only be provided with one tended lifeline; and

(d)    appropriate two-way communication with the diver is provided.

**45** When the diver is connected by a lifeline to a surface marker float, the appropriate surface support team should be in a position to render assistance in an emergency. If two divers are connected by a buddy line, only one marker float need be used.

*Use of compressed air or gas mixtures*

**46** Divers breathing a mixture of oxygen and nitrogen under pressure, whether compressed natural air or an artificial mixture, are at risk of both oxygen toxicity and nitrogen narcosis as the depth increases. The maximum depth for breathing mixtures of compressed air or oxygen and nitrogen is 50 metres of water. The recommended maximum partial pressures for oxygen are 1.4 atmosphere for SCUBA and 1.5 atmosphere for surface-supplied diving plant. This does not apply to therapeutic recompression.

*Exposure limits for surface-orientated diving*

**47★** Diving carries an inherent risk of decompression illness (DCI). The incidence of DCI drops if the length of time that a diver spends at any particular depth is limited. The depth/time limitations are reproduced in Table 1. Use of this table has resulted in a significant reduction in the incidence of DCI, and diving project plans should incorporate these maximum time limits.

**48** When breathing oxy-nitrogen mixtures with oxygen percentages higher than in natural air, the equivalent air depth should be established. It is this equivalent air depth that should be used to establish bottom time limits.

★ See Annex 5 for relevant industry technical guidance

**Table 1**  Maximum bottom time limitations for surface decompression (SD) and in-water decompression

| Depth | | Bottom time† limits (minutes) |
|---|---|---|
| *Metres* | *Feet* | *SD and in water* |
| 0-12 | 0-40 | 240 |
| 15 | 50 | 180 |
| 18 | 60 | 120 |
| 21 | 70 | 90 |
| 24 | 80 | 70 |
| 27 | 90 | 60 |
| 30 | 100 | 50 |
| 33 | 110 | 40 |
| 36 | 120 | 35 |
| 39 | 130 | 30 |
| 42 | 140 | 30 |
| 45 | 150 | 25 |
| 48 | 160 | 25 |
| 51 | 170 | 20 |

† Bottom time is the total elapsed time from when the diver is first exposed to a pressure greater than atmospheric, (that is when leaving the surface to the time (next whole minute) that the diver begins decompression (measured in minutes)). Divers should always take the lowest depth stop, for example, for 49 metres the 51 metres stop should be used.

*Water flow, intakes and discharges*

49★ Divers are vulnerable to water flow, suction or turbulence - whether natural or caused by water intakes or discharges. Measures to protect the diver should be part of a safe system of work, for example a permit-to-work system.

*Restricted surface visibility*

50 Restricted surface visibility may affect the safety of the operation, for example when diving in darkness, heavy rain or fog. The diving project plan should identify when an operation should be suspended because of restricted visibility.

*Weather*

51 Adverse weather conditions may affect the safety of a diving operation and the diving project plan should identify when an operation should be suspended.

*Underwater currents*

52★ Currents may impose limitations on a diver's operational ability and safety.

*Diving near remotely operated vehicle (ROV) operations*

53★ There are a number of safety considerations that should be taken into account when divers are working with, or in the vicinity of, ROVs. These include entanglement of umbilicals, physical contact, electrical hazards. Possible solutions include restricting umbilicals in length and employing guards and electrical trip mechanisms.

*Safe use of electricity*

54★ Divers often come into contact with plant, including battery-powered equipment, operated by or carrying electricity. Care should be taken to ensure that the divers and other members of the dive team are protected from the risk arising from the use of electricity, in particular from any shock.

*High-pressure water jetting*

55★ Even an apparently minor accident with this plant has the potential to cause a serious internal injury to the diver. Safe operating procedures when using such plant should be followed.

*Lift bags*

56★ The use of lift bags underwater can be hazardous, for example the uncontrolled ascent or descent of a load.

*Abrasive cutting discs*

57★ The adhesive used in cutting discs tends to degrade under water causing the discs to break during use. Only dry discs not previously exposed to water should be used, and only those discs required for use by a diver at any one time should be taken under water.

★ See Annex 5 for relevant industry technical guidance

*Oxy-arc cutting and burning operations*

58★ There are dangers in the use of oxy-arc cutting and burning underwater, for example explosions from trapped gases, and the trapping of a diver by items after cutting. Safe operating procedures should be followed.

*Diving from vessels*

59 Safe systems of work should be enforced to prevent divers from suffering injury from vessel propulsion systems, and must include exhibiting appropriate signs and signals.

*Flat-bottomed vessels*

60 Precautions to help the diver avoid disorientation when working beneath a flat-bottomed vessel should be considered.

**Breathing gases**

*Quantity of gases*

61 The quantities of gases required for diving operations, including primary, secondary and therapeutic treatments, should be calculated and procedures for the provision of them stated when planning a diving project.

*Quality of gases*

62 Procedures for checking and maintaining gas purity standards should be provided.

**Medical and physiological considerations**

*Liaison with a doctor*

63 The situation where a member of the dive team is injured or becomes ill but a doctor is not available at the work site should be considered.

*Diver monitoring*

64★ Supervisors should monitor divers' breathing patterns and receive oral reports from divers of their condition.

*Adjacent noisy operations*

65 There are potential problems for divers and the dive team exposed to high noise levels, for example from pile driving and concrete breaking. Noise reduction and hearing protection procedures should be used.

*Decompression illness*

66 The diving contractor should identify the arrangements in place for the treatment of any cases of decompression illness (DCI).

6(2), 8(1),(3)

★ See Annex 5 for relevant industry technical guidance

*Altitude changes after diving*

67* Guidance on travelling/flying after diving should be contained in the company's generic risk assessment. If these factors are relevant to a particular project they should be identified in the diving project plan.

*Thermal stress*

68* Excessive heat and cold can affect the health, safety and efficiency of divers and the dive team. Appropriate personal protective equipment and procedures should be provided to maintain thermal balance.

**Familiarisation**

69 When arriving at a dive site before the start of a diving project, all members of the dive team should familiarise themselves with the diving project, plant, and any other relevant details.

70 A familiarisation programme should be included in the diving project plan where it is appropriate for one to be carried out, for example a large and/or complex diving project. The personnel conducting any explanations or training should be identified and their names recorded. Satisfactory completion of the familiarisation programme by each individual in the dive team should be recorded.

71 The time required for familiarisation will depend on the experience of each individual and whether that individual has previously carried out the same job in that location or a similar job in another location.

**Use of checklists**

6(2), 8(1),(3)

72 A diving project will involve sequences, some of which may be complex, of different steps. There is a risk that steps may be omitted or taken out of sequence. A suitable way to ensure the thoroughness of such sequences is the use of prepared checklists that require relevant personnel to tick a box to demonstrate correct completion.

# Dive teams and associated working practice

*(3)   The diving contractor shall -*

*(a)   ensure that there are sufficient people with suitable competence to carry out safely and without risk to health both the diving project and any action (including the giving of first-aid) which may be necessary in the event of a reasonably foreseeable emergency connected with the diving project;*

## Dive teams

73    The diving contractor must specify the size of the dive team based on the details of the diving project and the risk assessment. There must be a sufficient number of competent and, where appropriate, qualified personnel to operate all the diving plant and to provide support functions to the dive team.

74    The diving contractor and the supervisor must satisfy themselves that a diver has the competences for the specific tasks required during a particular diving operation. On-the-job or other training may be necessary for individuals to gain competence. Where an inexperienced diver is gaining experience in a dive team the other team members and the supervisor will need to be aware of this and provide support.

## Overall management

75    The diving contractor should provide a clear reporting and responsibility structure in the diving project plan which takes into account that certain individuals, for example supervisors, have specific responsibilities that cannot be changed.

## Team size

76    The required size of the dive team will depend on the risk assessment which should take into account the number of hours to be worked each day, the type of diving, the diving plant and the techniques to be used, any decompression requirements, and the appropriate number required for safety.

77    The minimum team size normally required to conduct a dive safely within the scope of this Code is four - a supervisor, a working diver, a standby diver and a tender for the working diver (see paragraphs 79 and 80). Additional people may be required to operate or maintain specialised plant, such as winches, and to assist in an emergency.

78    However, a dive team of three - a supervisor, working diver and standby diver/tender - may be acceptable in controlled conditions in a swimming pool or a tank where there is no risk of entrapment and the management of an emergency has been considered. Controlled conditions in this context means that no aspect of the working environment can change without the specific authorisation of the supervisor. In such circumstances, when diving in swimming pools and tanks specifically in clear visibility, the standby diver can be dispensed with. However, a third person is needed on the surface to assist the supervisor with an emergency recovery of the diver.

The third person is part of the diving team and should not leave the immediate vicinity of the dive site while the diver is in the water unless sent by the supervisor to summon emergency assistance. The third person should be competent to perform such duties.

## Tenders

79    The diving contractor should be satisfied that the tender is competent. The tender should be familiar with the diving procedures to be used and the contingency and emergency plans for the project.

80    For umbilicals or lifelines that are tended from the surface, at least one tender is required for each diver in the water. For umbilicals tended from a basket or stage, one tender is required for each diver in the water.

## Standby diver

81    A standby diver should be in immediate readiness to provide any necessary assistance to a diver in the water.

82    The standby diver will normally be on the surface and should be dressed to enter the water, but need not be wearing a mask or a helmet. This equipment should, however, be immediately to hand.

83    When surface-supplied breathing apparatus is being used for carrying out diving operations under this Code it should also be used by the standby diver(s).

## Overlapping functions

84    Individuals in a dive team may carry out more than one duty, provided that they are competent and, if appropriate, qualified to do so and that their different duties do not interfere with each other or affect the safety of the dive team. For example, divers may carry out other associated duties while waiting to dive, such as acting as tenders or standby divers, or operating and attending to plant.

## Personnel not employed by the diving contractor

85    Personnel who are not employed by the diving contractor but who are considered for inclusion in the dive team must be competent for the work that they are going to do. They should be familiar with the diving contractor's procedures, rules and the diving plant that is to be used.

86    Arrangements for their involvement should be set out in the diving project plan together with details of their responsibilities and reporting line.

## First aid

87    The diving contractor is responsible for ensuring that enough people in each dive team have been trained to the required standard of first aid. For all diving projects under these Regulations, the required standard is the First Aid at Work standard, as defined by the Health and Safety (First-Aid) Regulations 1981 Approved Code of Practice.

88   All trainee divers undergoing a diver competence assessment will be taught and assessed for:

(a)   the first-aid qualification to the standard prescribed in paragraph 87. On successful completion they will be issued with a first aid at work certificate;

(b)   the reasons for and ways of giving oxygen. Such training will be provided at the diver training organisation. On successful completion, they will be issued with a certificate in oxygen administration.

89   Both these qualifications will be valid for three years. There is no legal obligation on divers to attend refresher courses or to renew the qualifications if they do not wish to do so.

90   For diving under this Code, the supervisor and at least one diver in each dive team should be qualified in first aid to the standard prescribed in paragraph 87. The supervisor should be responsible for arranging their duties so that one of them should be able to administer first aid, should it be needed, to a member of the dive team in an emergency.

91   The diving contractor's risk assessment, which should be carried out before the start of the diving project, should consider whether additional members of the dive team need to be qualified in first aid. In particular the assessment should take into account the type of diving to be undertaken, the tools and techniques to be used, the size of the dive team and the distance of the dive site from emergency services. The Health and Safety (First-Aid) Regulations 1981 Approved Code of Practice sets out additional advice for those areas where special additional training may be necessary to cover less common risks.

92   The diving contractor should provide first-aid equipment to the standard set down in the Health and Safety (First-Aid) Regulations 1981 Approved Code of Practice.

# Diving plant

*(3)   The diving contractor shall -*

*(b)   ensure that suitable and sufficient plant is available whenever needed to carry out safely and without risk to health both the diving project and any action (including the giving of first-aid) which may be necessary in the event of a reasonably foreseeable emergency connected with the diving project;*

**ACOP**

**93   The diving contractor must be satisfied that sufficient plant, suitable for the use to which it will be put, is provided for the diving project and that sufficient plant is available, whenever needed, which is suitable to carry out safely any action which may need to be taken in a reasonably foreseeable emergency.**

**94   Suitability can be assessed by the evaluation by a competent person, clear instructions or statements from the manufacturer or supplier, physical testing, or previous use in similar circumstances. All items of equipment worn by the diver should, wherever possible, be to international, European or national standards.**

**High-pressure cylinders and low-pressure vessels**

**95★   Gas cylinders should comply with all relevant statutory provisions.**

**Marking and colour-coding of gas storage**

**96★   Accidents have occurred because of wrong gases or gas mixtures being used in a diving project. The diving contractor should ensure that all gas storage units comply with the international, European or national standards of colour coding and marking of gas storage cylinders, quads and banks. Where appropriate, pipework should also be colour-coded.**

**Divers' breathing gas supply systems**

**97★   Each diver's breathing gas should be of the correct composition, temperature and flow for all foreseeable situations. This includes independent primary and secondary supplies. Gas supplies should be arranged so that interruption of supplies to one diver will not affect other divers' supplies.**

**98   Whatever type of breathing apparatus is in use, each diver should carry an independent reserve supply of breathing gas that can be quickly switched to the breathing circuit in an emergency. This should have sufficient capacity to allow the diver to reach a place of safety. If SCUBA is used the independent reserve supply should not be compromised if the primary supply fails.**

**Emergency breathing gas cylinders**

**99   When a diving basket is used by surface-supplied divers, emergency breathing gas cylinders should be supplied in the basket in a standard layout. This allows divers to access the cylinders rapidly in an emergency.**

★ See Annex 5 for relevant industry technical guidance

## Oxygen

100   Pressurised oxygen can fuel a serious fire or cause an explosion; it should therefore be stored and handled correctly. Any gas mixture containing more than 25% oxygen by volume should be handled as if it were pure oxygen.

## Communications

101   All divers in the water should have a communication system that allows direct voice contact with the supervisor on the surface and vice versa.

102   A hard-wired communication system is preferred because the effectiveness of a through-water communication system can be degraded by acoustic shadow, sediment, air bubbles, turbulence etc. Practical testing of the equipment in the operational location is recommended in order to ensure its effectiveness.

103   There are benefits to recording such communications and keeping the recording until the dive is successfully completed. For example, if an incident occurs during the dive the recording may help in any subsequent investigation.

## Lifting plant to carry personnel

104   Such equipment should be designed in accordance with other statutory provisions, international, European or national standards.

105   Particular selection criteria should be used for lift wires to carry personnel, including any wires for secondary or backup lifting. These wires should be non-rotating and have an effective safety factor in accordance with international, European or national standards. Further guidance is available in the Approved Code of Practice to the Lifting Operations and Lifting Equipment Regulations 1998.

## Winches

106*   Winches should be provided with independent primary and secondary braking systems. It is recommended for hydraulic winches that the secondary system operates automatically whenever the operating lever is returned to neutral or on loss of power. Both braking systems should be tested separately by a competent person.

107   Winches should not be fitted with a pawl and ratchet gear where the pawl has to be disengaged before lowering.

## Diving baskets and open-bottom bells

108   A basket or open-bottom bell, used in support of surface-supplied diving, should be able to carry at least two divers in an uncramped position. It should be designed to prevent the diver falling out and to prevent spinning and tipping. The basket should be fitted with suitable overhead protection and handholds.

109   Provision of a secondary means of recovering the divers should be provided.

* See Annex 5 for relevant industry technical guidance

Availability of compression chambers

110 The diving contractor has a responsibility to ensure the provision of facilities so that a diver can be recompressed in an emergency, should this be necessary. Treatment of DCI in a compression chamber should commence as soon as possible. The provision of a recompression chamber should be in accordance with the decompression procedures selected as part of the diving project plan.

111 In addition, the following minimum standards should also be applied:

(a) for dives with no planned in-water decompression and that are less than 10 metres the diving contractor should identify the nearest suitable operational two-person, two-compartment chamber. Under no circumstances should this be more than 6 hours travelling distance from the dive site;

(b) for dives over 10 and up to 50 metres with either:

- no planned in-water decompression; or

- with planned in-water decompression of up to 20 minutes,

a suitable two-person, two-compartment chamber should be no more than 2 hours travelling distance from the dive site;

(c) for dives with planned in-water decompression greater than 20 minutes a suitable, operational, two-person, two-compartment chamber should be provided for immediate use at the site of the diving project. The diver should be able to leave the water quickly and easily and be pressurised within the chamber to the appropriate recompression pressure as defined by the time in the decompression schedule being used. The controls of a surface compression chamber should only be operated by persons competent to do so. Such competence will be achieved by a combination of training and experience. The degree of supervision provided should reflect the experience of the operator.

112 In all cases where the recompression chamber is not located on the site, the diving project plan should include arrangements to ensure that in an emergency a diver will be able to be transported and recompressed to ensure, so far as is reasonably practicable, his or her safety. The diving project plan should record the suitable chambers which have been identified and the arrangements which have been made for emergency recompression throughout the course of the diving project.

Suitability of compression chambers

113* Two-person, two-compartment compression chambers should be suitable for the purposes intended and comply with the recognised standard appropriate to this Code.

Transporting an injured diver under hyperbaric pressure

114 A diving contractor who is responsible for transporting a diver to

* See Annex 5 for relevant industry technical guidance

21

hospital or other place under hyperbaric pressure should ensure that a competent chamber operator/supervisor accompanies that diver.

**Oxygen availability**

115   Oxygen should be immediately available at all locations covered by this Code, including those where there is a recompression chamber. Sufficient gas should be provided for the duration of a transfer of a diver to a recompression chamber, hospital or other place. It should be provided by a tight-fitting mask or by a mouthpiece with a noseclip.

# Maintenance of diving plant

*(3)  The diving contractor shall -*

*(c)  ensure that the plant made available under sub-paragraph (b) is maintained in a safe working condition;*

116  Diving plant is used under extreme conditions, including immersion in salt water. It should therefore be maintained, examined and tested regularly. It should be inspected immediately before use by a competent person to ensure that it is not damaged or suffering from deterioration.

**Planned maintenance system**

117  The diving contractor should establish a system of planned maintenance for plant. Maintenance arrangements should take into account both passage of time and usage. Details of the maintenance arrangements should be entered in the diving project plan. The arrangements should identify the item of plant, the date of the check, any limitations as to use, any repairs or modifications carried out and the signature of the competent person.

**Periodic examination, testing and certification**

118★ The frequency and extent of examination and testing required for all items of plant used in a diving project should be in accordance with relevant statutory provisions, and international, European or national standards.

**Cylinders used underwater**

119★ Divers' emergency gas supply cylinders and other cylinders used underwater can suffer from accelerated corrosion and must be regularly examined and maintained.

**Diving basket and wet bell lift wires**

120  Frequent immersion in water, shock loading, passing over multiple sheaves and so on can cause wear and deterioration to the lift wires if they are not properly maintained.

**Lift bags**

121★ Special requirements for the periodic examination, testing and certification of lift bags have been established. Manufacturers' maintenance instructions and testing requirements should be followed.

★ See Annex 5 for relevant industry technical guidance

# Supervisors

*(1) Only one supervisor shall be appointed to supervise a diving operation at any one time.*

**122 A supervisor must be appointed in writing by the diving contractor. If a diving project is taking place over such an area or time-scale that its operation cannot be controlled by one supervisor, then further supervisors should be appointed. Written appointments should clearly define the times and areas of control. The supervisor should have immediate overriding control of all safety aspects of the diving operation for which he or she is appointed.**

*(2) No person shall be appointed, or shall act, as a supervisor unless he is competent and, where appropriate, suitably qualified to perform the functions of supervisor in respect of the diving operation which he is appointed to supervise.*

**Suitable qualifications**

**123 A supervisor must be suitably qualified as a diver for the diving techniques to be used in the operation, or have acted as a supervisor of a diving operation in which the same diving techniques were used during the two-year period before 1 July 1981. For example, if a diving contractor is employing surface-supplied and SCUBA divers for a particular diving operation, it would not be acceptable to appoint a supervisor who was only qualified for SCUBA diving; the supervisor would have to be qualified in both surface-supplied and SCUBA diving.**

**124 Supervisors do not have to have a certificate of medical fitness to dive but should be qualified in first aid (see also paragraphs 87-92) and should be competent to manage a medical emergency.**

**Competence**

**125 The diving contractor must consider the competence of a person before appointing him or her as a supervisor. When considering competence, the diving contractor should consider such questions as whether the person is knowledgeable, practical, reliable; capable of conducting the diving operation in a safe manner; capable of managing members of the diving team appropriately; capable of acting sensibly in an emergency; and so on.**

**126 The diving contractor will be in a good position to decide on a person's competence if the person has worked for the company for some time. If the diving contractor does not know the person, it will be necessary for the diving contractor to make appropriate enquiries concerning the person's knowledge and experience.**

**Knowledge and experience**

**127 The supervisor must have adequate practical and theoretical knowledge and experience of the diving techniques to be used in the diving operation for which he or she is appointed. A person should only be appointed as a supervisor if he or she has:**

**(a) sufficient experience; and**

**(b) passed an approved diver competence assessment (see also paragraph 123).**

*(1)   The supervisor shall, in respect of the diving operation for which he has been appointed as supervisor -*

*(a)   ensure that it is carried out, so far as is reasonably practicable -*

*(i)   without risk to the health and safety of all those taking part in that operation and of other persons who may be affected thereby;*

**ACOP**

**Responsibility of the supervisor**

128   Supervisors are responsible for the operation that they have been appointed to supervise and they should only hand over control to another suitably qualified supervisor appointed for that diving project by the diving contractor. Such a handover must be entered in the diving operation record. Supervisors can only supervise that part of a diving project that they can safely and personally control, both during routine operations and in an emergency.

129   The supervisor with responsibility for the operation is the only person who can order the start of a dive. Other relevant parties, such as a harbour master, can, however, tell the supervisor to terminate a dive for safety or operational reasons.

130   A supervisor should be in control when a diver is under pressure in a surface compression chamber at the site of the diving project.

131   During diving operations from a vessel, the supervisor should liaise with other personnel, such as the vessel master. In such circumstances, the supervisor should recognise that the vessel master has responsibility for the overall safety of the vessel and its occupants.

132   To ensure that a diving operation is carried out safely, supervisors must conduct the diving operation in accordance with the requirements of the diving project plan and the site-specific risk assessment. They should:

(a)   ensure, as far as is reasonably practicable, that the operation that they are being asked to supervise complies with the requirements of this Code;

(b)   satisfy themselves, as far as is reasonably practicable, that the proposed dive site and the water and weather conditions are suitable;

(c)   ensure that the risk assessment is still current for the prevailing circumstances on the day of and during the dive;

(d)   ensure that they understand their own areas and levels of responsibility and who is responsible for any other relevant areas;

(e)   satisfy themselves that the personnel that they are to supervise are competent to carry out the work required of them and where appropriate hold a suitable and valid certificate. They should also check, as far as is reasonable, that these personnel are fit, and in possession of all necessary certificates, ie where appropriate, medical fitness to dive, diver's certificate and first-aid certificate;

(f) ensure that the diving project plan and arrangements for dealing with foreseeable emergencies are clearly understood by all those engaged in the diving operation. This would normally be ensured by carrying out a pre-dive briefing session with all those involved and, if appropriate, carrying out a rehearsal of the arrangements;

(g) check that the plant that they propose to use is adequate, safe, properly certified and maintained. They should ensure that the plant is adequately inspected by themselves or another competent person before its use. Such inspections should be documented, for example on a prepared checklist, and recorded in the diving operation record;

(h) ensure that the possible hazards from complex or potentially hazardous plant have been evaluated and are fully understood by all relevant parties and that, if required, training or familiarisation is given;

(i) establish so far as they are reasonably able that all relevant people are aware that a diving operation is to start or continue. They should also obtain any necessary permission before starting or continuing the operation, for example when working in or close to a lock or in a harbour;

(j) have adequate means of communication with any personnel under their supervision. So long as they have such communication they do not need to be able to operate physically every control under their responsibility. For example, a supervisor will be able to supervise adequately the raising and lowering of plant if there is a direct audio link with the winch operator, even though the winch may be physically located where the supervisor cannot see it or have ready access to it;

(k) maintain proper records of the diving operation. This must include the particulars in Annex 1;

(l) maintain the diving operation record throughout the diving operation for which they are appointed.

10(1)(a)(i)

## Regulation 11

*A supervisor may, whilst supervising the diving operation in respect of which he is appointed, give such reasonable directions to any person taking part in that operation or who may affect the safety of that operation as are necessary to enable him to comply with regulation 10.*

133 The supervisor is entitled to give reasonable orders in relation to health and safety to any person taking part in the diving operation. These orders take precedence over any company hierarchy. These orders could include instructing unnecessary personnel to leave a control area, instructing personnel to operate plant and so on.

# Divers

## Regulation 12

Regulation

12(1)(a)

*(1)   No diver shall dive in a diving project unless he -*

*(a)   has, subject to paragraph (2), an approved qualification which is valid for any activity he may reasonably expect to carry out while taking part in the diving project;*

## Regulation 14

Regulation

14(1)

*(1)   The Executive may approve in writing such qualification as it considers suitable for the purpose of ensuring the adequate competence of divers for the purposes of regulation 12(1)(a).*

ACOP

12(1)(a), 14(1)

**Qualifications**

**134   All divers at work must hold an approved diving qualification suitable for the work that they intend to do. A list of current approved qualifications can be obtained from HSE.**

## Regulation 13

Regulation

13(1)(a)

*(1)   No person shall dive in a diving project -*

*(a)   unless he is competent to carry out safely and without risk to health any activity he may reasonably expect to carry out while taking part in the diving project;*

ACOP

13(1)(a)

**Competence**

**135   Divers must be competent to do the work allocated to them within the diving project plan. A basic level of diving competence may be assumed from a diver who has an approved diving qualification. They should have a good understanding of diving physics and physiology and decompression. They should be able to recognise the signs and symptoms of diving-related illnesses in themselves and others and initiate appropriate treatment. They should be able to carry out a diver rescue, including the performance of resuscitation techniques. They should be able to initiate appropriate actions in the event of an emergency.**

Regulation

13(2)(a)

*(2)   Every person engaged in a diving project shall comply with -*

*(a)   any directions given to him by a supervisor under regulation 11;*

ACOP

13(2)(a)

**136   All people in the dive team have a responsibility to co-operate with the supervisor and to follow any reasonable directions and instructions that the supervisor gives.**

## Regulation 12

Regulation

12(3)(a)

*(3)   Every diver engaged in a diving project shall -*

*(a)   maintain a daily record of his diving;*

ACOP

12(3)(a)

**137   Divers' daily records (logs) must include the particulars in Annex 2.**

## Regulation 17

Regulation

17(1)

*(1)   Any certificate of training and any certificate of medical fitness to dive issued, or having effect as if issued, under the Diving Operations at Work Regulations 1981[a] ("the 1981 Regulations") shall have effect, subject to any conditions or limitations contained in any such certificate, as if it were, as the case may be, an approved qualification or a certificate of medical fitness to dive for the purposes of these Regulations.*

*(a) SI 1981/399 as amended by SI 1990/996 and SI 1992/608*

ACOP

17(1)

**138   The main and restricted HSE part certificates issued under the Diving Operations at Work Regulations 1981 are still legally valid and do not have to be exchanged for the new certificates.**

**139   Transitional certificates issued under regulation 15 of the Diving Operations at Work Regulations 1981 are still legally valid.**

**140   Certificates issued by the Manpower Services Commission (MSC) and the Training Services Agency (TSA) are still legally valid, but may be exchanged for the appropriate HSE certificate.**

# Medical checks

*(1)   No diver shall dive in a diving project unless he -*

*(b)   has a valid certificate of medical fitness to dive.*

**141   All divers at work must have a valid certificate of medical fitness to dive issued by an HSE medical examiner of divers. The certificate of medical fitness to dive is a statement of the diver's fitness to perform work underwater, and is valid for as long as the doctor certifies, up to a maximum of 12 months.**

**142   Where an annual medical examination is carried out less than a month before the expiry of the current medical certificate to dive, the start date of the new certificate may begin from the expiry date of the current certificate.**

**143   Trainee divers who train while at work must hold a certificate of medical fitness to dive before they begin training. This will help potential divers to be aware of any health problems that may affect their employment prospects or long-term health, should they continue to dive. The pre-training medical examination contains the same elements as the annual medical assessment with the addition of such investigations as blood group and so on.**

**144   Every diver, or person who is likely to be subject to hyperbaric conditions as routine rather than in an emergency, must have a valid certificate of medical fitness to dive.**

*(1)   A certificate of medical fitness to dive is a certificate from a medical examiner of divers (or from the Executive following an appeal under paragraph (4)) that the person issuing the certificate considers the person named in the certificate to be fit to dive.*

**145   The medical examination and assessment look at the diver's overall fitness to dive. These include the main systems of the body - cardiovascular system, respiratory system and central nervous system - as well as the ears, nose and throat, vision, dentition, and the person's capacity for exercise.**

*(1)   No person shall dive in a diving project -*

*(b)   if he knows of anything (including any illness or medical condition) which makes him unfit to dive.*

**146   People who dive in a diving project and who consider themselves unfit for any reason, for example, fatigue, minor injury, recent medical treatment, must inform their supervisor. Even a minor illness, such as the common cold or a dental problem, can have serious effects**

on a diver under pressure, and should be reported to the supervisor before the start of a dive. Supervisors should seek guidance from the diving contractor or the company's medical adviser if there is doubt about a diver's fitness to dive.

147[*] People who dive in a diving project who have suffered an incident of DCI should record details of the treatment they received in their daily record (log book). They should show this to the supervisor before taking part in their first dive after the treatment in order that a check can be made of their fitness to return to diving. Supervisors should seek guidance from the diving contractor or the company's medical adviser if there is doubt about a diver's fitness to dive.

# Regulation 15

(6)    In this regulation, "medical examiner of divers" means a medical practitioner who is, or who falls within a class of medical practitioners which is, for the time being, approved in writing by the Executive for the purposes of this regulation; and any such approval may be given generally or restricted to any class of diver or dive.

148   HSE approves doctors to carry out diving medical examinations and assessments. These medical examiners are selected for approval based on their training in diving physiology and their knowledge of diving. This approval is for a limited period, usually for one or two years. Details are available from HSE.

[*] See Annex 5 for relevant industry technical guidance

# Particulars to be included in the diving operation record

1   Name and address of the diving contractor.

2   Date to which entry relates and name of the supervisor or supervisors (an entry must be completed daily by each supervisor for each diving operation).

3   Location of the diving operation, including the name of any vessel from which diving is taking place.

4   Names of those taking part in the diving operation as divers and other members of the dive team.

5   Approved Code of Practice that applies to the diving operation.

6   Purpose of the diving operation.

7   Breathing apparatus and breathing mixture used by each diver in the diving operation.

8   Time at which each diver leaves atmospheric pressure and returns to atmospheric pressure plus his bottom time.

9   Maximum depth which each diver reached.

10   Decompression schedule containing details of the pressures (or depths) and the duration of time spent by divers at those pressures (or depths) during decompression.

11   Emergency support arrangements.

12   Any emergency or incident of special note which occurred during the diving operation, including details of any decompression illness and the treatment given.

13   Details of the pre-dive inspection of all plant and equipment being used in the diving operation.

14   Any defect recorded in the functioning of any plant used in the diving operation.

15   Particulars of any relevant environmental factors during the diving operation.

16   Any other factors likely to affect the safety or health of any persons engaged in the diving operation.

17   Name and signature of the supervisor completing the record.

18   Affix company stamp (if appropriate).

# Details to be included in the diver's daily record (log)

Names and addresses should be printed and in block capitals.

1    Name and signature of the diver.

2    Date to which entry relates.

3    Name and address of the diving contractor.

4    Name and signature of the supervisor(s) for that dive.

5    Location of the diving project, including the name of any vessel from which diving is taking place.

6    The maximum depth reached on each occasion.

7    The time the diver left the surface, the bottom time, and the time the diver reached the surface on each occasion.

8    Where the dive includes time spent in a compression chamber, details of any time spent outside the chamber at a different pressure.

9    Breathing apparatus and breathing mixture used by the diver.

10    Any decompression schedules followed by the diver on each occasion.

11    Any work done by the diver on each occasion, and the plant (including any tools) used in that work.

12    Any episode of barotrauma, discomfort or injury suffered by the diver including details of any decompression illness and the treatment given.

13    Any emergency or incident of special note which occurred during the diving operation.

14    Any other factor relevant to the diver's health or safety.

15    Affix company stamp after the daily record has been signed by the diver and the supervisor(s).

# Glossary of terms and abbreviations

**Competence**

Competence means having a combination of training, knowledge and experience such that the person can do the job required in a safe and efficient manner.

**Hazard**

A hazard is something with the potential to cause harm. This may include water, environmental factors, plant, methods of diving and other aspects of work organisation.

**Permit-to-work system**

A formal written system used to control certain types of work which are identified as involving significant risk.

**Risk**

A risk is the possibility that someone or something will be harmed by an identified hazard. The extent of the risk includes the numbers of people who might be affected by the risk.

**Risk assessment**

A risk assessment is a careful examination of what may cause harm and an evaluation of precautions that can be taken to prevent harm.

**ADC**

Association of Diving Contractors

**AODC**

Association of Offshore Diving Contractors (superseded by ADC and IMCA from 1 April 1995)

**DCI**

Decompression illness

**DVIS**

Diving Information Sheet

**DMAC**

Diving Medical Advisory Committee

**HSC**

Health and Safety Commission

**HSE**

Health and Safety Executive

**IMCA**

International Marine Contractors Association

**MSC**

Manpower Services Commission

**ROV**

Remotely operated vehicle

**SCUBA**

Self-contained underwater breathing apparatus

**SD**

Surface decompression

**TSA**

Training Services Agency

## Major legislation

This legislation covers all industries and may be relevant to diving projects. This list is not exhaustive.

1   *The Health and Safety at Work etc Act 1974.*

2   *Health and Safety (Display Screen Equipment) Regulations 1992* set out requirements for work with visual display units.

3   *Management of Health and Safety at Work Regulations 1999* require employers to carry out risk assessments, make arrangements to implement necessary measures, appoint competent people and arrange for appropriate information and training.

4   *Manual Handling Operations Regulations 1992* cover the moving of objects by hand or bodily force.

5   *Personal Protective Equipment Regulations 1992* require employers to provide appropriate protective clothing and plant for their employees.

6   *Provision and Use of Work Equipment Regulations 1998* require that plant provided for use at work including machinery is safe.

7   *Workplace (Health, Safety and Welfare) Regulations 1992* cover a wide range of issues such as ventilation, heating, lighting, seating and welfare facilities.

8   *Employers' Liability (Compulsory Insurance) Act 1969* requires employers to take out insurance to cover their liability for accidents and ill health sustained by their employees.

9   *Health and Safety (First Aid) Regulations 1981* cover requirements for first aid.

10  *Health and Safety Information for Employees (Modifications and Repeals) Regulations 1995* require employers to display a poster telling employees what they need to know about health and safety.

11  *Control of Noise at Work Regulations 2005* require employers to take action to protect employees from hearing damage. The Regulations now apply offshore.

12  *Electricity at Work Regulations 1989* require people in control of electrical systems to ensure they are safe to use and maintained in a safe condition. The Regulations now apply offshore.

13  *Health and Safety (Training for Employment) Regulations 1990* set out how certain people being trained for employment should be treated for the purposes of health and safety law.

14  *Chemicals (Hazard Information and Packaging for Supply) Regulations 2002* require suppliers to classify, label and package dangerous chemicals and provide safety data sheets for them.

15  *Construction (Design and Management) Regulations 2007* cover safe systems of work on construction sites.

16    *Control of Substances Hazardous to Health Regulations 2002 (as amended)*
      require employers to assess the risks from hazardous substances and take
      appropriate precautions.

17    *Reporting of Injuries, Diseases and Dangerous Occurrences Regulations 1995*
      require employers to notify certain occupational injuries, diseases and
      dangerous events.

18    *Carriage of Dangerous Goods and Use of Transportable Pressure Equipment
      Regulations 2007* regulate the transport of pressurised gas cylinders.

19    *Lifting Operations and Lifting Equipment Regulations 1998* include any
      equipment used at work for lifting or lowering loads.

# Sources of information

| Reference | Title | Paragraph(s) |
|---|---|---|
| DVIS5 | Exposure limits for air diving operations | 47 |
| AODC 055 | Protection of water intake points for diver safety | 49 |
| AODC 047 | Effects of underwater currents on divers' performance and safety | 52 |
| AODC 032 (Rev1) | Remotely-operated vehicle intervention during diving operations | 53 |
| AODC 035 | Code of Practice for the safe use of electricity under water | 54 |
| IMCA D042 | Use of battery-operated equipment in hyperbaric conditions | 54 |
| DMAC 03 | Accidents with high pressure water jets | 55 |
| AODC 049 | Code of Practice for the use of high pressure water jetting equipment by divers | 55 |
| IMCA D016 | Underwater air lift bags | 56 |
| DVIS1 | General hazards (Section on abrasive cutting discs) | 57 |
| DVIS1 | General hazards (Section on prevention of explosions during oxy-arc cutting operations) | 58 |
| MaTR133 | Investigations into the damage caused to a diver's helmet by an explosion during oxy-arc conditions in the North Sea | 58 |
| DMAC 02 | In-water diver monitoring | 64 |
| DMAC 07 (Rev1) | Recommendations for flying after diving | 67 |
| DMAC 08 | Thermal stress in relation to diving | 68 |
| AODC 010 (Rev1) | Testing, examination and certification of gas cylinders | 95 |
| ADC 5/95 | Minimum criteria to be met by a surface supply inland/inshore air diving panel for diving operations in the UK | 96 |
| AODC 028 | Divers' air gas supply | 97 |
| DVIS3 | Breathing gas management (Section on divers' gas supply systems) | 97 |
| DVIS2 | Diving system winches (Section on air-driven winches) | 106 |

| Reference | Title | Paragraph(s) |
|---|---|---|
| ADC 8/97 | Minimum specification for surface compression chambers for inland/inshore diving | 113 |
| IMCA D018 | Code of Practice on the initial and periodic examination, testing and certification of diving plant and equipment | 118 |
| AODC 037 | Periodic examination of bail-out bottles | 119 |
| IMCA D016 | Underwater air lift bags | 121 |
| DMAC 013 (Rev1) | Guidance on assessing fitness to return to diving | 147 |

The future availability and accuracy of the references listed in this publication cannot be guaranteed.

Printed and published by the Health and Safety Executive    C4    01/08